MAKING YOUR MARK

The publication of this book marks the tenth year that Supon Design Group has been "making its mark" in graphic design. The firm's success is due, in large part, to its clients— those who have entrusted Supon Design Group to "make their marks" great.

©1998 by Design Editions
A division of Supon Design Group, Inc.

All rights reserved. Copyright under International and Pan-American Copyright Conventions.

No part of this book may be reproduced, stored in a retrieval system, or transmitted in any form or by any means, electronic, mechanical, photocopying, recording, or otherwise, without prior permission of the publisher.

While Supon Design Editions makes every effort possible to publish full and correct credits for each work included in this volume, sometimes errors of omission or commission may occur. For this we are most regretful, but hereby must disclaim any liability.

All work represented has been produced either for Supon Design Group or commissioned by Supon Design Group's clients. In some cases, work represented may include photography, illustrations, or other images owned and copyrighted by our clients or their vendors. All logos, trademarks, and images are the property of their respective owners. These may include our clients, their vendors, or the estates of specific individuals.

All of this book is printed in four-color process. A few of the designs reproduced here may appear to be slightly different than their original reproduction.

ISBN 1-889491-08-X
Library of Congress Catalog Card Number 98-70120

Distributed to the trade in the United States, Canada, and Mexico by:
BOOKS NIPPAN
1123 Dominguez Street, Unit K
Carson, CA 90746
Fax 310-604-1134

Published by:
DESIGN EDITIONS
1700 K Street, NW, Suite 400
Washington, DC 20006
Phone 202-822-6540
Fax 202-822-6541

Acknowledgments:
PROJECT AND CREATIVE DIRECTOR
Supon Phornirunlit

JACKET DESIGNERS
Khoi Vinh
Soung Wiser

BOOK DESIGNERS
Soung Wiser
Sara Wretborn

EDITORS
Wayne Kurie
Greg Varner
Stephen Smith

PRODUCTION COORDINATOR
Colm Owens

PHOTOGRAPHER
Oi Veerasarn

Printed in Korea

MAKING YOUR MARK

Establishing Unique Corporate Identities with Graphic Design

SUPON DESIGN GROUP

table of contents

6   Making marks—Then and now

8   About supon design group—
An insider's view

10   A deliberate approach

14   The icon

46   The type

72   The look

Visit our Web site at www.designeditions.com

making marks then and now

Identity design has been around for thousands of years. The earliest logos and trademarks date back to prehistoric times, and even then, they answered one or more of the same basic questions—who owns this? Who made it? What is it?

Corporate identity today tells you the same things. The manufacturer, or owner, describes it in the most attractive terms possible before transferring ownership to someone else for an agreed-upon price. The core functions of an identity system are unchanged, though products, and their means for delivery, have become more complex with time.

In its earliest incarnation, identity design probably resembled the modern use of monograms. Prehistoric hunters may have marked their weapons with signs indicating ownership. Even in preliterate societies, an "X" or a cross denoted a kind of signature. In English, the application of identifying marks to livestock became known as *branding*. To *brand,* indeed, comes from the Old Norse word meaning to *burn*. Later, a complex system of identifying signs was developed for use in heraldry. Ancient Greek and Roman pottery was marked with symbols representing the manufacturer, an early manifestation of the modern phenomenon of the store brand. This shirt is from Store A; that one, while similar, is from Store B. Does it really matter which is which? Yes, and to some people, a great deal. That's the power of the brand.

Even today, in places where department stores are unheard of, a lettermark or a typographic logo might still be recognized without being fully understood as such. Widely known typographic marks are recognized before they are really read. Their distinctive typefaces and other identifying elements work in concert to hasten recognition.

All of this goes to suggest the manner in which identity design operates. It's faster than reading, preliterate, almost subconscious. Identity design is a personal shorthand used by companies to communicate as broadly as possible.

The longevity and persistence of identity design indicates the depth of the human need it fulfills. At some point, somebody noticed that burning a mark into an animal's flesh was the most permanent and foolproof means of identification. Branding techniques were used around the globe by the time knights recognized each other by the symbols on their helmets and shields in the Middle Ages. Many of today's logos—and even company names—date back to this complicated system of heraldic marks.

Heraldry made explicit the modern connection between design and value, with signs representing different aristocratic families and cadency marks indicating the birth order of the sons. Today, the relationship between design and value can be restated in the following equation: Excellent design suggests a corresponding excellence at the organizational or product level.

But how is excellence in design measured? Not in aesthetic terms alone, for the simple reason that people don't agree on aesthetic standards. Instead, excellence is measured by consensus of informed opinion and by effectiveness. If a logo or trademark is too complicated, or doesn't convey the necessary information, it hurts a product or company no matter how attractive it may be.

Contemporary identities answer the same old questions, but go further, to make statements about specific qualities of the companies or products they represent. Logos routinely make claims regarding such characteristics as speed, comfort, reliability, modernity, or technological ability.

These qualitative or tonal components of identity are generally organized around opposing polarities: technological vs. humanistic, contemporary vs. traditional, luxurious vs. practical, and so on. Creating a mark that successfully straddles both ends of a familiar spectrum—for example, for a technology company that wants to stress its humanistic side is a true designer's feat.

From spear-marking and sheep-branding to the sophisticated corporate identity systems of today, the fundamentals haven't changed. We still need designs that speak on our behalf. Logos typically distinguish letterheads, business cards, and numerous other applications, with each presenting its own subtle challenges for effective deployment.

Blending the earliest ingredients of identity systems—monograms, branding symbols, heraldic signs—in a modern synthesis, we can trace their survival in contemporary logos, both iconographic and typographic, and their use in creating overall "looks"—coordinated systems of images making qualitative claims about a person, product, company, or event.

Concluding our historical survey of identity, it is fitting to remember the derivation of the word, logo, from the Greek word for *speech* and *logic:* The logo speaks to viewers, but its use must also make sense.

about supon design group
an insider's view

As soon as they walk through the studio door, visitors to Supon Design Group can see they are some place unique...some place different. The jester's throne at the reception desk is one clue. The vibrantly colored sculptures and prints are another, and so is the laughter coming from one of the conference rooms. The office mascots—two toy dogs named Pica and Cricket—further the sense of unexpected delight.

The studio's friendly, personable image turns out to be an accurate reflection of reality. One reason for this, as many members of the Supon Design Group crew will tell you, is that "it's a great place to work." The environment itself is creative, which only makes sense, given the nature of the business. And the staff is eclectic and diverse—some people crossed continents on their way to work here; others crossed city blocks. This cosmopolitan quality both reflects and encourages our open-mindedness, and it nourishes our problem-solving abilities.

We know how to have a good time, but we also know how and when to get down to business, as office visitors can infer from the steady hum of activity. In short, it's a unique atmosphere, fast-paced and dynamic, where the mood can swing quickly from crazily intense to intensely crazy—just what you'd expect from a hard-working, diverse, and talented group.

In the words of one Supon Design Group designer, "We have amazing capabilities in-house." We put a lot of skill at the client's disposal, along with a willingness to try any technique, on or off the computer, to get the desired result. Our extraordinary success is partly the result of giving the nearly twenty designers on staff the room to grow and the encouragement to express themselves creatively. It's also due to our knowledge of our clients and their problems. We are skilled at the art of putting ourselves in others' shoes.

Our basic philosophy is that design should strike a balance between form and function. We challenge the forms as much as we can—pushing here, extending there, depending on the job—while always respecting the integrity of the function.

Another unique aspect of our office has to do with the variety of our clients, who are even more diverse, in the aggregate, than we are. They come from the realms of sports, education, high technology, entertainment, food and beverage, public policy, and many more, bringing an equally wide array of projects and outlooks. We design identity systems, publications, Web sites, T-shirts, and everything in between. Because our projects are varied, designers never get bored or go stale. Exposure to differing business problems and their solutions keeps designers interested and cultivates versatility. Designers also appreciate the high quality of the projects on which they have the opportunity to work. "It's inspiring to know your stuff might be seen by thousands of people," said one.

Perhaps the most unusual thing about Supon Design Group is the way the creative team functions as just that—a *team*, working together to solve the client's problems. Everyone from design interns to the creative director can affect the outcome of a project. Often, everyone on staff works on the same project, at least in the early stages. The final presentation to clients frequently incorporates the ideas of many staff members. Clients may interact with only one person—typically, an account executive or art director—but they are never relying on just one person's creative output.

A word that most often comes up when staff members talk about Supon Design Group is "family." We socialize outside the office from time to time, of course, but we also help each other work in a way that can best be described as caring and familial. And like any large family, we even have our share of sibling rivalry—designers are teammates, but they're in a friendly competition with each other to find the best solution. All of this means clients can be sure they're getting our best. And, in the end, that is our sole objective.

a deliberate
approach

As designers, we make it our business to situate a product or company in the public mind through the use of images. Taken together, these images comprise an identity. The logo is the key image in such systems, the cornerstone without which the entire structure collapses.

Design is not arbitrary; it's rooted in a client's overall marketing strategy. If a logo looks good but doesn't say anything about the company it represents, it's not a good logo. Our job as designers is to be creative—to convey the client's messages, but in a less prosaic way than simply restating them.

Crazy, wacky design for a corporate client won't work. An identity must reflect where a company is today—as well as where it expects to be tomorrow. We want our work to have a long shelf life, to outlast trends. Supon Design Group is known for logos that are accessible and inviting, exciting, distinct, and full of energy. Our identity work is not so straightforward that its meaning is obvious, nor so full of intrigue that it is obscure. Simplicity is the hallmark of a good identity. Even when a business is complex—perhaps especially then—one simple mark must carry a great deal of information. A successful mark says the most with the least, in the cleanest, most elegant way.

But it's a mistake to try to capture too many themes in one logo. If a mark says even one thing well, that's an accomplishment. If it successfully frames its main idea with one or two additional qualifying ideas, that is truly remarkable. The logo seldom needs to do all the work by itself because it's rarely seen in isolation. Context goes a long way toward filling in the gaps.

Research precedes development. We study the company and its objectives, paying some attention to what its competitors are doing, to formulate an idea of the type of identities currently in use within the industry in question. Does the client want something similar or purposefully distinct? Frequently, every designer on the Supon Design Group staff works on an identity, at least in these initial stages. This guarantees that a variety of approaches will be considered. First, we brainstorm on paper, trying idea after idea in sketches, until something clicks. Often, it's something unexpected—lucky accidents happen to those who are ready and able to take advantage of them.

But concept and execution are two very different things. Once we determine a direction, we're only halfway home. Some of our favorite logos express their meaning in the way they are rendered. For example, a polished, smooth mark may work for an all-natural clothier. But perhaps it would be stronger if it shared some of the rough, textured qualities of the product. Attention to detail makes all the difference. There are also technical requirements which a logo must meet. It must reproduce well at all sizes and—the acid test, for clients who want to fax or photocopy their stationery—it must work in black and white.

Once a logo is approved, the next step is its translation to an increasingly varied set of applications. Letterhead, envelopes, and business cards are essential for even the smallest operations. Secondary applications may include additional business forms, brochures, and signage. Further applications, such as truck sides, menus, and packaging, for instance, may be equally essential given the needs of a specific industry or locale. In order to avoid insuperable problems in the future, the requirements for each project must be considered early in the design process.

Increasingly, new-media applications are making their way into the promotional portfolios of many businesses. This is partly a matter of keeping up with competitors, a classic case of the "everybody-else-has-one-so-I-want-one-too" syndrome. But there are better reasons. Audiences are beginning to demand Internet presence from companies and brands. And the World Wide Web has the capacity to communicate more directly and more economically to a greater number of people than traditional materials ever could. Be it in print or online, clearly conveying one's business is the founding objective of any corporate identity.

But core messages rarely remain stagnant over time. As corporate capabilities and cultures change, identity must as well. Your company hasn't stood still. Its identity must not either.

We invite you to flip through the following pages, featuring samples of work by Supon Design Group. Though the designs span nearly a decade, note that each solution retains a timeless quality, still an engaging visual and effective communication piece. Whether for a mom-and-pop shop or a Fortune 500 corporation, all of these works demonstrate creative ways of "making your mark."

Supon Phornirunlit is owner of Supon Design Group, Inc., where he serves as creative and art director. Since founding the company at the age of 24, he and his design team have earned over 700 industry awards, including recognition from every major national design competition. The studio specializes in logo and identity design, and has created such graphics for numerous high-profile organizations. Supon Design Group has clients ranging from the U.S. to Europe to Asia, including such notables as IBM, Coca-Cola, the Discovery Channel, and the U.S. Postal Service. The firm's work has appeared in numerous publications, including *Graphis, Communication Arts, Print, Step by Step,* and *How.* Supon regularly speaks and judges at various organizations and schools.

Visit the Supon Design Group Web site at www.supon.com

the icon

i·con, n. 1. A picture or image. 2. A sign or representation that stands for something by virtue of a resemblance or analogy to it; symbol.

Iconographic logos pictorially refer to a product or business. This reference can be direct (resemblance) or indirect (analogy). On an indirect level, even typographic logos are iconographic, or are recognized as icons after repeated exposure.

Icons operate by tapping into the powerful human capacity for recognition that precedes literacy. In this realm, the sign of the pretzel instantly brings Danish bakeries to mind, and a neon cocktail glass is shorthand for "lounge." Once viewers learn the simple visual codes of this kind, they can function well within a contextual system.

In addition to such straightforward denotation, icons can also be metaphors. A rock can signify stability; a mountaintop can suggest excellence. Context becomes even more important for interpreting logos of this sort—while they are straightforward at the pictorial level, their true referent is disguised, and becomes transparent only with familiarity.

Iconographic references can also be simply arbitrary. At this level, a camel or a cowboy stands for a cigarette brand. Even here, however, the camel refers directly to the brand name, and the cowboy, it could be argued, is a metaphorical reference to the rugged outdoors supposedly favored by those who smoke a certain type of cigarette. Where commercial art is concerned, as in real life, categories frequently blur.

Arbitrary references split into two types. First are the so-called "found" or representational icons with no obvious association (except, often, the name) to the product or company referent, such as the camel or the shell. The second type are abstract marks without any initially recognizable pictorial referent—original symbols designed specifically to represent a company or product.

Certain visual motifs have been frequently adapted for use in iconographic logos. These include animals, eyes, keys, globes, ships, stars, flags, and hearts. Needless to say, these items are all powerfully symbolic and loaded with association. Icons can also be descriptive diagrammatically. An abstract wave, for example, can be pressed into service by makers of ultrasound equipment.

Icons are frequently combined with type, and just as often used in isolation. There are no hard-and-fast rules regulating their use. But the more metaphorical or abstract icons become, the more ways they can be perceived, which is not to say they're less effective than straightforward marks. In fact, as people's perceptions are based on their own unique experiences, such abstract marks may be even stronger than clear-cut ones; viewers will internalize meanings (therefore perceptions) of a company or product logo, making it even more relevant to their own needs.

The mysteries of how individual people see the same things in different ways are cause for celebration more than despair—after all, this is the foundation on which designers build their work in the first place.

PARALYZED VETERANS OF AMERICA

Victory and patriotism are combined in this solution for the National Veterans Wheelchair Games. The raised arms of the athlete convey pride, while the flag above the figure makes the link with veterans.

INTERNATIONAL GAY AND LESBIAN FOOTBALL ASSOCIATION

This design for a World Cup '97 event is an enhanced execution of the client's existing concept, using the U.S. Capitol building to indicate the championship game's Washington, D.C., location. Rainbow-colored lines represent gay pride, as well as the motion of the ball.

ISL MARKETING

The mark for the "Under 17" youth soccer tournament held in Ecuador offered a global look, not tied to a particular nationality. Playful without being too childish, this logo relies on typography to tell the story.

US TENNIS ASSOCIATION

The day before the US Open begins has been designated Arthur Ashe Kids' Day, when kids have a chance to participate in tennis clinics with celebrities. An event logo characterized by simplicity and action was required. The inclusion of both male and female figures indicates the co-educational nature of the program, while the ribbon is an allusion to AIDS and to Arthur Ashe. The star is a subtle reference to the celebrities who appear at the event.

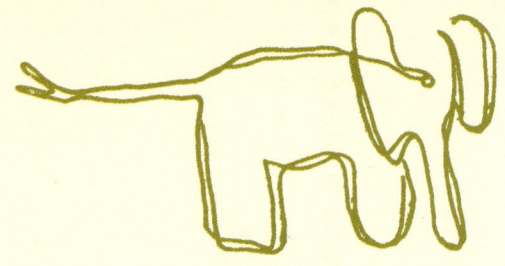

WANA ZOO

WANA ZOO

Carefully planned contrasts make this system appealing for a broad audience. Colorful drawings of animals convey the nature of the zoo to children—even those who are still too young to read—while the black background adds a grown-up sophistication suggesting that the zoo is fun for adults, as well.

WANA ZOO

WANA ZOO

WANA ZOO

A similar juxtaposition involves the contrast of the classical typeface with the playful, free forms of the animals. These applications demonstrate how the various elements in an identity system—foreground and background, color, type, shape and line—can work together to reach a broad target audience.

JAVELIN GROUP

The Javelin Group is a marketing firm that specializes in bringing together corporations with sporting events for sponsorship opportunities. Its logo combines a classical figure treated in a modern way with a solid foundation of type. Together these convey dynamism, speed, and reliability.

GRAND PALACE FOODS INTERNATIONAL

The label for this bottled water was designed to work well in upscale markets. The delicacy of the illustration and the modesty of the figure's pose combine to suggest freshness and purity.

THE COCA-COLA COMPANY

A disposable cooler containing soft drinks was emblazoned with the instantly recognizable ribbon and name. The fun-loving figures suggest parties, picnics, and sporting events, all probable usage venues for this product.

NATIONAL TRUST FOR HISTORIC PRESERVATION

A different neighborhood each year is presented with the Great American Main Street Award for its contribution to historic preservation. The rectilinear bars of type frame a street scene on a sunny day, capturing the simplicity of small-town life, but in an inventive style.

PLANET CALLED EARTH

A retail chain specializing in nature-related items, Planet Called Earth sought a friendly, earthy image. Naturalness was the most important quality to be conveyed, an objective realized with the hand-drawn look.

V/S SPA AND MASSAGE CLUB

In this logo for a health spa, the lines of the figure's hair flow into those of the water, conveying harmony, wellness, and connection with nature, as well as refreshment.

AMERICAN WHOLESALE MARKETERS ASSOCIATION

An exposition themed "Solutions in Houston" focused on ways to integrate technology, people, and (inventory, shelf, warehouse) space to further the sales and distribution of candy. Elements suggesting each of these aspects are combined into a unified mark which formed the central focus of each of these marketing pieces.

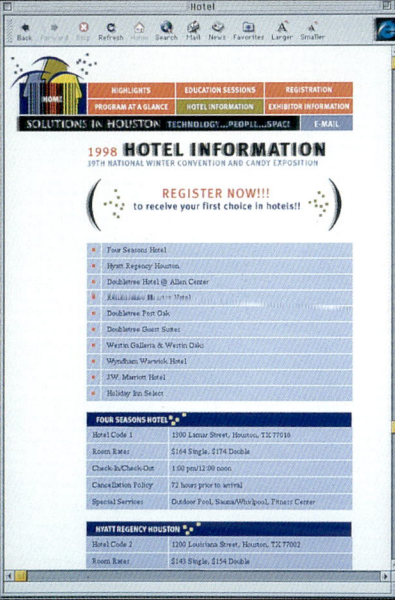

MUSEUM OF JUNK

This unique store is a playful cross between a museum and a junk shop, where customers can buy collectible treasures or inexpensive replicas. The logo, applied to everything from shopping bags to a Web site, fuses

NATIONAL COMMUNITY AIDS PARTNERSHIP

The way AIDS unites diverse populations is stressed in this mark, with the black-and-white figures linked in a circle to suggest community and helping hands. The play between positive and negative suggests that both seropositive and seronegative individuals are joined in the fight against AIDS.

NATIONAL ASSOCIATION FOR THE CARE OF THE HOMELESS

"Home is where the heart is," according to the well-known proverb. This solution for a nonprofit organization shows that compassion can make a metaphorical home.

CREATIVE SQUARE

Designed for a commercial and residential space planner, this mark presents a clear encapsulation of the business. A square shape defines a space, and the different ways of showing the edges of the square represent creative planning.

DESIGN EDITIONS

A tongue-in-cheek solution for a publisher of graphic-design books shows a doodle, the everyday emblem of creativity. This suggests the publisher's playful personality and area of expertise.

PARADISE WILD

This retail store specializes in gift items related to animals and nature, with the intent of increasing environmental awareness. The jungle-inspired solution accomplished this, and added drama to stationery, shopping bags, signage, and other items.

NARAI COMPANY

In keeping with the playful product name, Good Doggie, a lighthearted illustration in bold, lively colors was chosen for these labels. Even when these cans are turned the "wrong" way on store shelves, the product is recognizable—instead of heads, canine tails appear.

[opposite]
NARAI COMPANY

Various color combinations were calculated to stand out on store shelves, was used for new flavors in this line of cat food. The product logo is the same color on every can to solidify brand identity. The overall feeling is fun and free—words many cat lovers would use to describe their frisky, playful felines.

DISCOVERY COMMUNICATIONS, INC.

Graphically connecting people with technology, a magenta border and full-color icons memorably represent the online branch of this telecommunications company. The existing identity of the Discovery Channel was the recognizable take-off point for this solution.

BYZENTINE

A logo and identity were created for Byzentine, a T-shirt company comprised of several different market divisions. The sun graphic is a classic, in this case done in a timeless illustration style; and the type is hand-drawn—not machine-made—so the overall feel of the identity is representative of the historical era for which the company is named.

BYZENTINE

CANYON produces T-shirts and other outdoor wear for Byzentine. Each application features an illustration of a canyon as it would appear in a different light: dawn for the envelope, day for the clothing tag, and night for the letterhead. The reverse of each piece carries yet another canyon image, this time photographic.

Its hand-drawn lettering and illustrative-style graphic give PACIFIKA an organic, even exotic look—appropriate for this division of Byzentine which creates T-shirts with playful beach and water motifs.

TUESDAY GIRL is a Byzentine division which creates T-shirts for teen and pre-teen young ladies. The brightly colored, whimsical illustration, undulating type, and pink paper stock all are designed to appeal to the clothing's target market.

WASHINGTON COURIER

Partial sketches combine to convey the Washington, D.C., location, and to show that this messenger service has the city covered. Short, quick brushstrokes suggest the speed with which they make their deliveries.

WARDS

To communicate the philosophy of an organization supporting the professional care of animals in research, the right combination of sentiment and practicality was necessary. The logo clearly emphasizes tenderness and compassion, while the content stresses the necessity of animal testing—albeit always humanely.

FRESH MARKET

In the labeling system for this line of pre-cut, ready-to-cook produce, the classic, softer lines were intended to appeal to urbane, health-conscious consumers. This system revitalized the standard plastic packaging.

**GREEN CITY
MARKET & CAFE**

This logo combined three icons from a much larger set created for this natural foods emporium. Color was used to appeal to a young target audience, while the wholesome foods were stressed with an earthy, organic look.

**INTERNATIONAL
FOOD POLICY RESEARCH
INSTITUTE**

An illustrative symbol which can be interpreted both as a group of people working together and an edible crop forms the mark for IFPRI, an organization created to help developing countries devise policies to improve agricultural production and distribution.

HORTICARE

Both elegant and whimsical, this logo combines a concern for aesthetics and function to convey the nature of this landscape design firm.

**UNITED STATES
BOTANIC GARDEN**

The Capitol's famous dome combines with a flower in this effective pictorial shorthand, framed by the agency name. Bold marks like this are especially suitable for application at various sizes, from smallest to largest.

DIVERSE HANDEL

A retailer of trendy, offbeat housewares imported from Europe, this client required an identity that would speak to its upscale customers. The solution was a very contemporary vignette of a home interior.

ATLANTIC OCEAN PAINT

The logo for this Indonesian paint manufacturer shows a figure holding a trident, a spear associated with the god of the sea. The trident has special meaning for the company's founders: An antique specimen was found in the ground at the firm's headquarters, and became the company symbol.

WEARHOUSE

Recycled paper and nuances of color used in this labeling system suggest the "natural" quality of this upscale line of athletic socks. Various sports, including weight-lifting, track and field, and racquetball, are depicted in a series of illustrations, where horizontal lines convey high energy.

INTERNATIONAL GAY AND LESBIAN FOOTBALL ASSOCIATION

The logo for IGLFA, the sponsor of the gay and lesbian World Cup, features a friendly individual spanning the globe. This emphasizes the international comraderie among the tournament's various soccer teams. A subtle pink triangle in the name restates the membership's orientation.

PEOPLE FOR THE AMERICAN WAY

A five-point star aptly represents this grass-roots organization which fights to protect the liberties promised all Americans by the Bill of Rights. The different renderings of each of the star's points suggests the vast diversity of peoples and issues for which PFAW works every day.

WESTERN POLICY CENTER

A unique portrayal of stars and stripes—derived from the U.S. flag—elegantly represents this public-policy corporation which works to advance U.S. interests in Greece, Turkey, and Cyprus.

XYZ PRODUCTIONS

"The Murder Show" television series features a logo that immediately conveys the subject matter of this whodunnit: a chalk outline of a corpse on pavement.

ZUCKERMAN BROTHERS

The stone arch has its origins in ancient Roman architecture—a fitting representation for the logo of this residential real estate developer whose new homes are at once classic and elegant.

ART DIRECTORS' CLUB OF METROPOLITAN WASHINGTON

Paper played an important role in this identity system, as did several dramatically high-contrast black-and-white photographs. This one-color job was very inexpensive to produce, a requisite of the client.

the type

type, n. A printed character or characters used in a system of writing.

In a typographic logo solution, the name of a company or product is employed directly into its mark. This can be its full name or just an abbreviation, even an acronym. Such use of type in a logo to convey a message—either alone or in combination with an icon—generally depends on simple visual repetition to build recognition for the name. For many organizations, the use of their name, especially proper names, signifies responsibility and pride. John Smith, the owner of the hypothetical John Smith Enterprises, has a lot riding on the integrity of his work. "I did this," such a logo proclaims, "and you can trust me." (All logos do precisely this, of course—it's just a matter of degree.)

Identity systems in general, and iconographic logos in particular, routinely collapse the name of a product or company into a picture. Typographic solutions reverse this standard equation, in that they collapse the image into the name, bringing the word back into the foreground.

Usually, of course, the entity's name has been established by the time a designer is invited to create its logo, but sometimes naming products or corporations is part of the assignment itself. This, in fact, is the ideal scenario: As an integral part of the name-generation team, the designer can judge a particular name on—among other criteria—its ability to be portrayed graphically. To be sure, creating a typographic logo involves devoting some original thought to both the name and its message. Only then can a designer appropriately embody these elements into a mark that works.

It's often possible to manipulate the letterforms to suggest certain properties of a company or product. A young, dynamic, high-growth company named Charge, for instance, would generally want these qualities conveyed through its logo. Such an powerful personality could be portrayed in the form of a symbol combined with type or purely typographically. In the latter solution, one can visualize the letterforms of the company's name increasing in size until they culminate with the ultimate letter exploding in an electric spark. Such a design could be described as a neatly mimetic representation verging on the pictorial—or, at least, relying on pictorial modes of thought. It's a case of visual logic applied in the verbal realm.

It is worth remarking on the correspondence between the way names represent companies or products and the way icons perform the same function. Descriptive names are, in fact, the verbal equivalents of representational icons. And just as icons can rely on metaphor and association, so can names: The fictitious appellation "Fresh and Good" for a bakery suggests wholesome breads made with all-natural, high-quality ingredients. As its name is so telling, its visual mark need only make a slight suggestion in this direction to cap off a very strong, and positive, image.

Synthetic names (the heretofore meaningless combination of letters to create an interesting-sounding name) as well as names combining numbers may also be good candidates for typographic solutions. Handwritten script adds a special dimension to typographic logos, typically using the idea of the human touch to suggest either refinement or heightened naturalness, depending on a script's formality (or lack of it). Again, it's a one-two punch, combining the power of words with the strength of images.

ADVENTIST HEALTHCARE MID-ATLANTIC

This healthcare consortium's symbol needed to convey reliability, professionalism, and quality. The expressive range of a strong, simple, one-letter mark is suggested here.

ASHBURY CAPITAL, LLC

A very classic, refined style is appropriate for this financing company's mark. The leaf forming the A's crossbar suggests a tree that's strong and stable—desired characteristics of any capital company.

ANDRUS FOUNDATION

This arm of the American Association of Retired Persons awards grants for gerontology research; it's logo demonstrates once again how a single letter can take on a very different personality depending upon the design.

ANDREW PARIS

This fashion designer wanted a symbol that would lend him the cachet of his namesake, Europe's capital of style. The combination of the letter "A" and the Eiffel Tower in a single mark was the inspired solution.

ATWATER COMMUNICATIONS
304 Lamond Place · Suite 200 · Alexandria, VA 22314 · 703.

ATWATER COMMUNICATIONS
304 Lamond Place · Suite 200 · Alexandr

ATWATER COMMUNICATIONS

For this provider of writing and public relations work, a dynamic swash as the letter's crossbar reflects the cutting-edge capabilities the firm offers clients.

GRAND PALACE FOODS INTERNATIONAL

When a logo and packaging were needed for a new caffeinated-water beverage targeting men, a large plastic bottle was selected as the right container, while light, clean typography and a clear label echo the simplicity of the product.

GRAND PALACE FOODS INTERNATIONAL

For packaging for Pure, a caffeinated-water beverage targeting women and upscale consumers, this small, blue-tinted glass bottle seemed a natural choice. Light, clean typography and a clear label echo the simplicity of the product.

**BUGS AND BEES
TOY STORES**

When appropriate, typography can be very playful. A kind of visual pun takes place in this whimsical solution for a toy company, where the letter "B" and its mirror image also form the body of a bug.

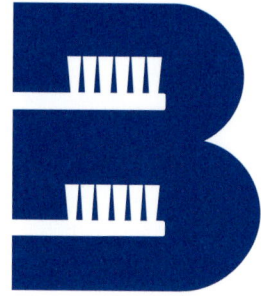

STEVEN T. BUNN, DDS

In this mark for a general family dentistry office, the pair of toothbrushes in the "B" describe the business. The friendly feel is purposeful, suggesting that dental work is not the horror that many believe.

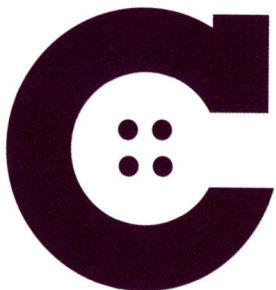

CHARLES BUTTON COMPANY

The placement of four holes in the center of the circle implied by the "C" turn the letter into a no-nonsense, crystal-clear icon for the product.

HARRIS CHAIR CENTER

By surrounding the lower-case "h" in a darker field, this solution conveys the solidity of the company, and functions both as an icon and as an initial for the company's name.

SPECIAL OLYMPICS

The 30th anniversary of the Special Olympics warranted a celebratory logo of its own. Depicting the spirit, pride, and athleticism of the athletes, this solution blends varying typographical styles and imagery.

GUNNISON

This Internet support company is on the cutting edge of emerging technologies. Its logo, a letter "G" enveloping two peaks, is a clever reference to Gunnison, Colorado, a Rocky Mountain resort town favored by the company's founder. The river or road formed by the reversed-out angle of the "G" subtly suggests moving towards new areas of technology.

GIANFAGNA MARKETING & COMMUNICATIONS, INC.

For a firm specializing in direct marketing, advertising, and public relations, this logo solution can be called minimalist. Some may see a "G," others may not. Either way, the message is clear: The firm is forward-looking and provides strategic direction to its clients.

THE REDMON GROUP

In this typographic treatment for a developer of interactive, multimedia software products, the "r" casts a shadow to form the letter "G," suggesting both a solid business foundation and the transformative aspects of multimedia.

AQUA VITAE

An Asian beverage distributor, Aqua Vitae wanted an elegant and upscale mark. The design features a very abstract "A" and "V." Both letterforms are delicately woven into a fluid motif suggesting water, the basis for the company's name and products. The stationery design gives dimension and movement to the mark.

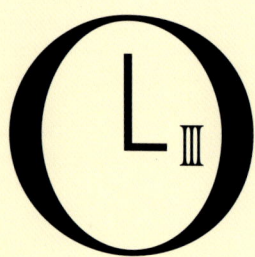

LOUISE OWEN III

The sides of an "O" were widened to suggest a watch face in this elegant solution for a watchmaker. Her creativity is suggested by the clever positioning of each typographic element.

ULMAN PAPER BAG COMPANY

The addition of a handle to the letter "U" turns it into a descriptive icon representing a paper-bag manufacturer. The size of both elements of this mark was carefully manipulated—if the letter had been a little smaller, or the handle had been wider, it wouldn't have worked as well.

VENTEK CAPITAL

The logo for this firm which provides financial resources to small- and medium-sized businesses was meant to be somewhat "edgy," and appeal to those with an entrepreneurial spirit. Its combination of a "V" and "C" into a single symbol is unique.

WALSH WALLPAPER COMPANY

Sometimes, as in this solution for a wallpapering service, a small alteration in one area of the logo transforms the whole into an extraordinarily effective commercial mark.

LINDA KLINGER

This professional writer and editor's initials are tucked into an emblematic tool of her trade. Different typefaces were used for the "L" in the identity's various applications, as a way of conveying the creativity and variety she offers clients.

MUSEUM OF SHOES

This proposed shoe store will display the actual footwear of famous people and will sell both reproductions of these as well as regular brands of shoes. Its initials are used to create a column in this elegant, playful mark.

  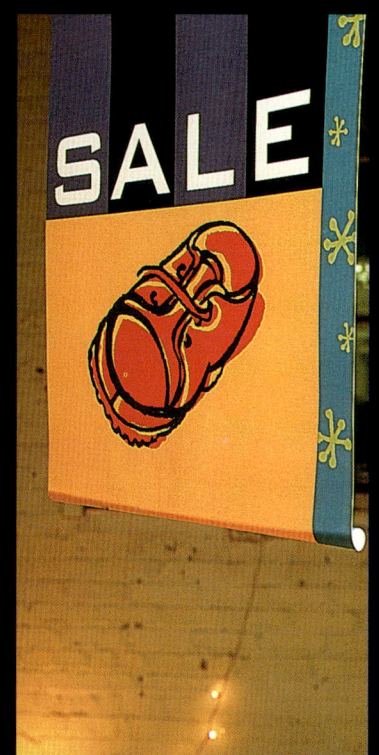

MUSEUM OF SHOES

Packaging and signage displayed throughout the store expand on the graphics and identity begun with the logo.

DATACAST

Datacast is a digital broadcasting service that uses conventional television signals to transmit digital information and multimedia content to PCs. This flow of information is represented in the altered "As" of this logotype.

DATACAST

TELEWORX

The solution for this telecommunications consulting and software development firm uses a bold, red "X," a yellow "O," and red-and-yellow swash to add visual interest. The "X" motif is used throughout the company's product line to further differentiate the indentity from that of competitors.

VERICOM SYSTEMS

This computer systems firm wanted a logo that would convey its reliability and solidity. The letter coming out of the box is a graphic presentation of the integrated services it offers; the overall effect is clean and high-tech, but not cold.

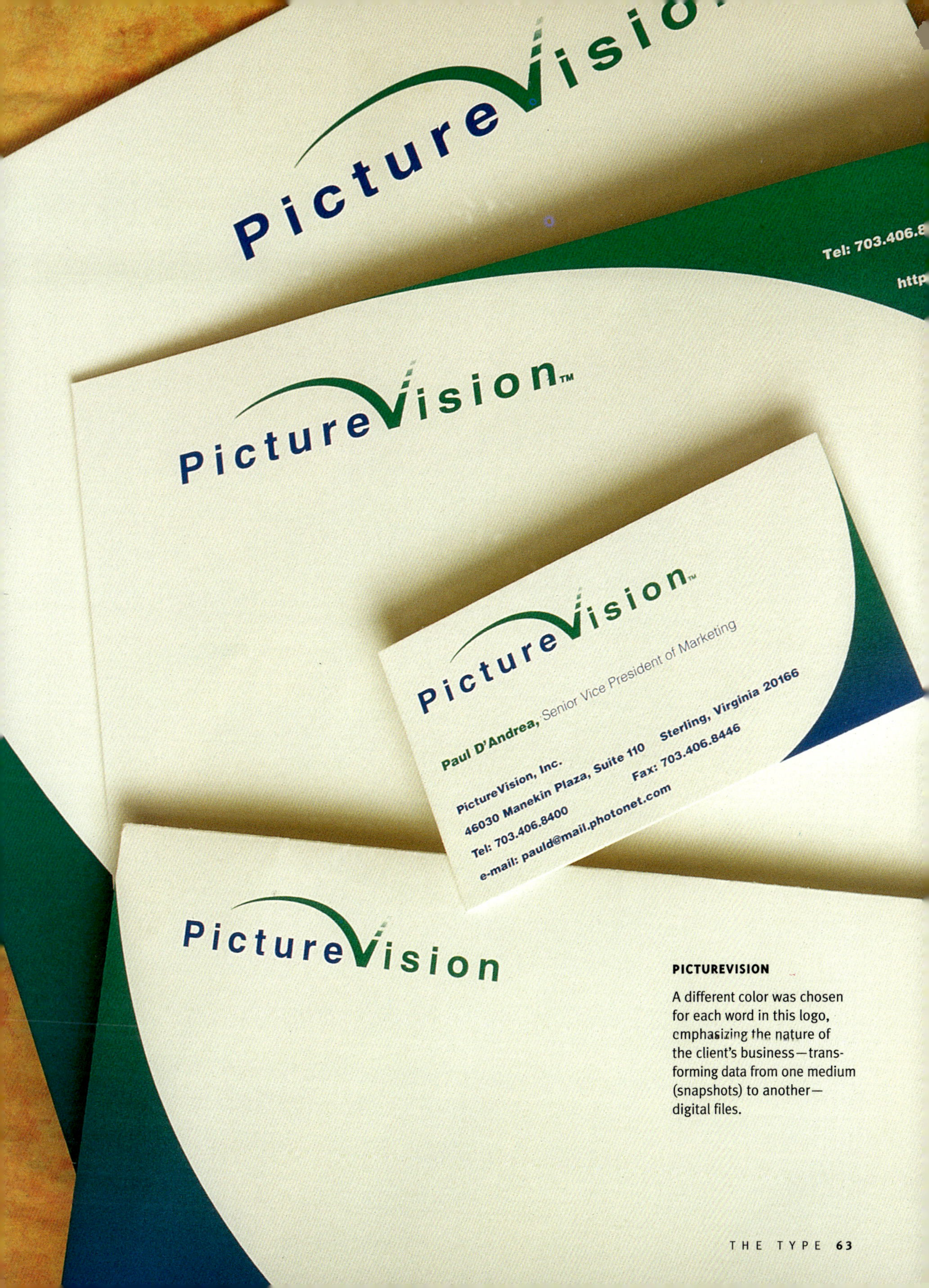

PICTUREVISION

A different color was chosen for each word in this logo, emphasizing the nature of the client's business—transforming data from one medium (snapshots) to another—digital files.

THE TYPE 63

GRAND PALACE FOODS INTERNATIONAL

A simple and elegant label harmonizes with the graceful curves of this bottle of Paradise Rice Wine. The minimalist style reflects the drink's Asian origins.

AMERICAN ASSOCIATION FOR CHILDREN'S HEALTH

The client did not want the mark for its Campaign for Kids and Families to be illustrative. The perfect solution involved using dramatic typography spelling out the words "kids" and "AIDS" to set the right tone and mood.

INDIGO AT GREAT FALLS

This restaurant, located in Great Falls, Virginia, features contemporary, American cuisine. The ultimate "o" of its name transforms into a leaf in the logo, suggesting the natural foods and ingredients offered. Each of the letterforms, in fact, is hand-drawn, adding to the identity's personal touch.

SPACE ADVENTURES

Rocket rides are just one of several exciting, space-related travel and recreational options offered by Space Adventures. The company's logo features an "A" masquerading as a rocket's parabolic flight path over the curvature of the Earth.

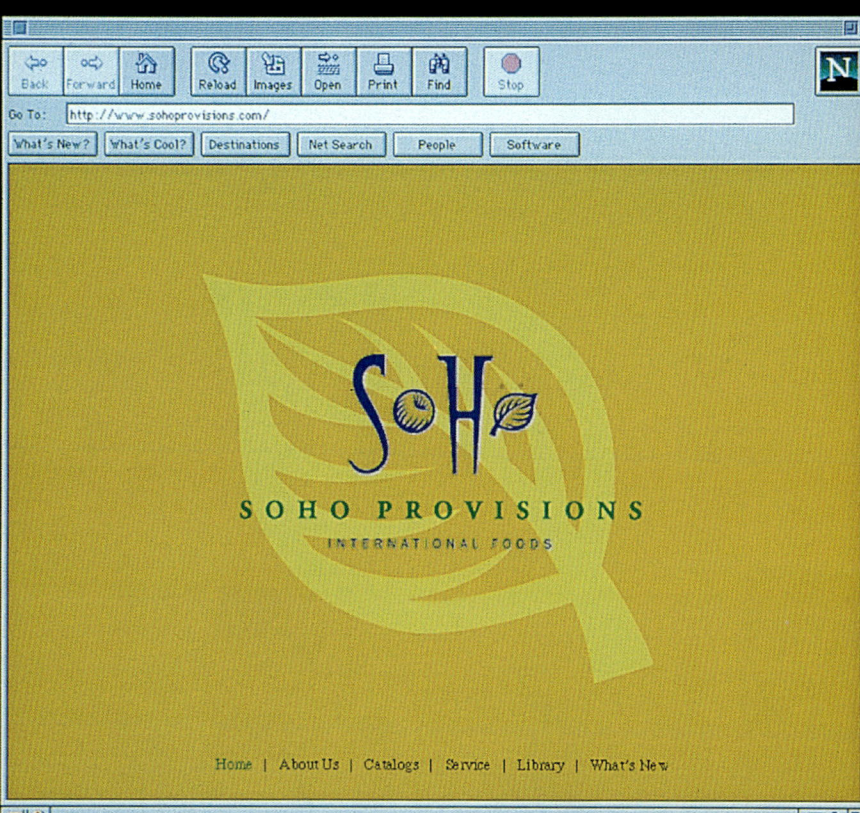

SOHO PROVISIONS

Exotic foods from around the globe are available through SoHo Provisions. The company is friendly and ecologically concerned therefore the company's logo and other applications work to convey this message. Graphics of leaves and fruit appear throughout, giving the identity—even the high-tech Web site—a "natural" feel.

SOHO PROVISIONS

The various product brands, including bread crumbs, coffee, and saffron shown here, each carry through the company's identity. Colorful stickers differentiate standard packaging on some items.

GRAND PALACE FOODS INTERNATIONAL

A line of light, regular, and thick soy sauces, Gobéy is sold in upscale gourmet shops. The bottles were given an elegant shape, an unusual small size, and were topped off with highly stylized labels and hang tags.

U.S. POSTAL SERVICE

"Celebrate the Century" is the theme of a 100-year retrospective of stamps issued by the U.S. Postal Service. A scalloped edge, reminiscent of stamp perforations, frame an elegant "100" entwined with a celebratory ribbon.

THE U.S. DEPARTMENT OF AGRICULTURE

This typographic treatment implies a square. The abstract image makes reference to agriculture's fields, and positions the federal organization's abbreviated name above the horizon. Since it is often used in smaller applications, this logo needed to be bold and clear.

PGA TOUR

The association of pro golfers launched a campaign entitled "The First Tee" in order to appeal to the masses, markets not generally thought of as golfers. The spinning globe/ball balancing on the tee suggests the diversity and international scope of this effort.

the look

look, n. The way in which a thing appears; aspect.

A logo is seldom used in isolation. Instead, it is deployed as part of an overall system of coordinated images, or incorporated into an entire campaign. Increasingly, identity design is also about creating an overall "look."

The look wraps images with a recognizable tone of voice, creating a strong network of associations. It encompasses color scheme, signage, architecture, and other elements. Using the visual clues provided by the look, we can tell instantly whether we're eating lunch in one fast-food restaurant or another, or learn who is sponsoring a sporting event or concert. Primarily concerned with tone, the look leaves no questions unanswered as to the feelings it is intended to evoke. At this emotional level, the logo itself is secondary—people don't have to see it directly to get the message.

The logo can take a back seat in the overall look partly because of the relative fullness of the visual environment, and partly because the look brings the associative and emotional content of the identity to the fore. The visual motif of an iconographic logo—animals, stars, keys, etc.—will usually be amplified and extended in the look; indeed, results may be disastrous if it is not. The mismatch of logo and look is like mounting noir drama on a musical set; to successfully do so requires surpassing delicacy and skill.

Normally, of course, the look will grow organically from a logo, the way all other elements of an identity will depend on the same source as both inspiration and anchor. If an identity system is a family of images, then the look can extend the family by marriage—other systems of images can be joined to an identity, broadening its power or creating something new. And like a marriage, the look can be annulled when the campaign or event has ended.

The look, in fact, is often invented for temporary use. IBM's sponsorship of the 1996 Olympic Games in Atlanta, or the Smithsonian Institution's traveling 150th anniversary exhibition, required the creation of a look to visually convey the necessary messages to audiences. Both of these had short shelf lives.

Ultimately, the look is about credibility and authority. "We have achieved a level of seriousness and importance," it declares, "and we have the power and the knowledge to create a total visual environment for your information and enjoyment." Used to convey sponsorship, it says, "We present this event because we share your interest in it."

As one would expect, given its emotional content, the messages a look can transmit vary widely. The look is an exciting and flexible instrument—it can shout or whisper, laugh or sing—and its power is still being explored.

WOLF TRAP

Reflecting this renowned outdoor theater's devotion to the arts, a hand-drawn look was essential for its promotional campaign. This illustration was created freehand; elements of this scene were used in various applications, from bus backs to brochures to clothing.

THE GEORGE WASHINGTON UNIVERSITY

Recruitment materials designed to convey the innovative character of The George Washington University were calculated to appeal to both potential applicants and their parents. The school's urban environment is emphasized along with its academic quality. Bright colors suggest fun and excitement, balanced with the "seriousness" of the black. The layout presents text in manageable "chunks" of information. Always, the richness and diversity of life at GW is stressed.

THE LOOK 77

THE ASSOCIATED PRESS

For the 150th anniversary of the Associated Press, the "AP 150" campaign was created, incorporating the news organization's existing logo into the commemorative pieces. The first item designed was the poster, whose look was then translated to numerous other applications. Through subtle changes in type and graphics, the identity characterizes AP in three ways: past, present, and future.

THE LOOK 79

SMITHSONIAN INSTITUTION

The look for the traveling exhibition commemorating the Smithsonian's 150th anniversary adapted the familiar Smithsonian sunburst logo, splitting it into four parts: In one quadrant, the original icon was featured, while the other three sections were used for photographically depicting the exhibit's three themes—discovering, imagining, and remembering.

SMITHSONIAN INSTITUTION

This look was applied throughout the exhibit on entrances and signage. It was also used on T-shirts, shopping bags, and other applications.

IBM

The blue stripes of IBM's existing corporate logo were integrated with figures of athletes to convey the company's sponsorship of the 1996 Atlanta Olympic Games. This look was used in applications ranging from small, mouse pads and lapel pins, to large, such as banners and bus wraps.

NEWSEUM

At Newseum, the world's only interactive museum of news, visitors learn about the relation between freedom and the press. A full-scale marketing identity was designed around a pre-existing logo. The extensive layering of photos and graphics suggests the depth of issues, information, and activities available at the high-tech site.

US TENNIS ASSOCIATION

For use on T-shirts and other products for sale at the US Open, cool, bright, sophisticated graphics were created, targeting an upscale market. Designs focused on several themes, including New York City, the international aspect of the tournament, and the game of tennis itself. Some graphics were done in a semi-abstract style; others were hand-drawn. Humor was used in some, while others took on an urban edge. The goal was to create a range of designs to appeal to the event's diverse enthusiasts.

BLACK ENTERTAINMENT TELEVISION

This brochure contains foldouts for each of BET's four networks. These are meant to convey the diversity of

BLACK ENTERTAINMENT TELEVISION

With an already strong presence in the cable TV industry, BET sought to expand its affiliate base, strengthen existing markets, and broaden ad sales. The resulting affiliate sales kit design included images promoting its youth, sports, news, and general programming on a demo tape, pocket folder, letter, and brochure.

[below]
BLACK ENTERTAINMENT TELEVISION

Bet on Jazz appeals to a more upscale demographic so its look is more subdued. Photos of jazz greats are featured throughout this moody brochure.

HOST MARRIOTT FOR RONALD REAGAN WASHINGTON NATIONAL AIRPORT

Graphic counter panels were designed for each of the tenants in Ronald Reagan Washington National Airport's food and beverage area. Four different styles were developed from which each tenant could choose the look it favored. These were then customized to each tenant's colors and food selection.